I0420849

THE FUNDAMENTALS

OF

WINNING IN POLITICS

(POLITICS ROSARY)

DEDICATION

I dedicate this book to the WORLD, and mostly AFRICA

COPYRIGHTS

TABLE OF CONTENTS:

CHAPTER ONE

INTRODUCTION:

In the face of this ever-rising chaotic wave in politics, political rejuvenation has become very necessary in the face of this ugly political upheaval worldwide.

The reason I wrote this book- the fundamental of winning in politics (Politics rosary) is to address the very huge and thick darkness (injustice) and malevolence in politics at many parts of the world, and mostly in Africa. Politics in Africa causes many politicians excruciating skin deep sacrifices. This is a BIG injustice among politicians that must be addressed to ensure reliable electoral processes and meaningful development by our governments.

Politics is not a dirty game and an issue of do or die affair. Therefore, an attention and sense of urgency must be giving to politics and other politically inclined issues that would give us niche for victories and fast economy development.

One of the subject matters also discussed in this book is how to triumph over all kinds of myriad dull moments that have populated and pervaded world politics.

Political mandate is given to us by God. This equals strength and authority which you put all commitments with pleasure but many of our politicians are stressed in our electoral processes.

In my own usual BIG way of saying and doing things, political mandate is a very BIG assignment we don't play with because it connotes government.

If you willingly obey and do coherently what is written in this book, you will certainly have the knowledge of how to win in politics and take delivering of your political mandate without paying an excruciating price for something not personal, and still fumbling, and swaying.

This book taught "Political mandate and the fundamental principles of winning and sustaining in politics. This book will put you in a state of being a political giant in world politics. You are mandated not to be defeated.

The reason many fail and mess up in politics is because they are not trained on how to win and to be an ever winning politician, and they do not know how to win, & nobody has taught them how to pass political tests and exams from their examiners (voters) for their conquest.

WHY YOU MUST READ THIS BOOK

(1) With this Book, you should able to learn and do politics free from intense excruciating sacrifices.

(2) You will learn the fundamental principles of wining in politics.

(3) The book will help us reduce politics of greed and misconducts, and bloody.

(4) This book has the capacity to prepare us in pursuance of our political mandate without a fear of defeat and hurting others.

(5). It will help us to curtail and exercise authority and wage war against corruption to the minimum as you will certainly win when you apply the fundamental principles of politics in this book

A wise man said, "Two incidents of note happened in my life when I was young. The first incident was in 1964 when I was at the University. At that time, the University had an exchange program with Michigan State University, U.S.A to sent brilliant students to the U.S.A. during summer to know more of America.

We all looked forward to qualify, but then we had to do some tests and pass before we could be selected".

This wise man was a distinction student in mathematics and he had enough experience on all kinds of mathematics examinations and had never failed mathematics, because he was taught how to solve mathematics problem and he passed.

Unknown to him, there was a final test outside mathematics which was a dinner party set before him and others but he failed because he was not trained how to pass or win on that test.

The table was set before them and they gave them a bowl of soup and a roll of bread each. The wise man grabbed the bread according to how he told the story; he dipped it in the soup and started eating. There was a man there who was taking notes. He waited until his mouth was filled that he could not talk and then asked him the question, "What would you do when you get to America?" Because his mouth was filled, he could not answer properly and the examiner took note.

After the meal, it was tea-time. Because the tea was very hot, he began to take it with the spoon provided. And at the end of the party, "he failed; "I could not understand why I failed", he said. I got to know more about table etiquette; I failed because I did not know how to pass. Nobody told or taught us in advance the things to know and how to pass".

There are several people who when going through life career they fail ultimately because they did not know how to pass table etiquette. Note! Politics has its etiquette.

When you are told and taught in advance how to win or pass, you will certainly win without losing. You will easily win or be selected because you had known what is expected of you to win in advance.

I do not want you to fail again. If you had failed before, there is another opportunity for you to pass after reading this book politics etiquette.

If you had not participated in politics before, this time you will know the reasons you have to and with the help of this book, you will know how to win and sustain it, rule, and keep winning without skin deep pain.

CHAPTER TWO

WHAT IS POLITICAL MANDATE?

In this current world of civilization and politics globalization, it is very difficult to succeed in politics without having a political mandate and agenda. Political mandate is mighty.

Political mandate is a divine calling into an under taken and authority on the platform of politics. The concern of this book is how to run to obtain political mandate and to address the injustice in Africa and World politics. The injustice in question, causing some politicians to be wicked and stealing in the public office is revealed and addressed in this book.

A mandate in this concept is explained in various ways and in different forms but they all stand to mean one thing.

A mandate is the heavenly authority give to a person to do something he or she is created for by God in the platform of politics. It is an official task given to a person from the time of conception to birth and growth to maturity. "It is an official order given to

somebody to perform a particular task"
(Oxford Advanced Learner's Dictionary
7th Edition).

Political mandate is authoritative order
to act for others. It is a command to act
and represent others.

There are various forms of mandate:

1. Statutory mandate

2. Corporate mandate

3. Religion or divine mandate and a
   Political mandate

All mandates in whichever form they
are presented and represented, they

are all divine-mandates because nobody can receive anything on earth except it is released to him from heaven.

Everybody has a reason or a purpose of being born to the planet, "earth". We are all born and packaged for a peculiar assignment or mandate (purpose).

Mandate can either be preventive or permissive. It is preventive when its intention is to bring certain happening or event to an end for instance when a set or group of people suffering under a political siege or slavery is to be stopped. You could be that kind of person mandated to bring to an end the affliction of his people – preventive political mandate brings to an end certain happening.

Political mandate is a permissive mandate when it marks the beginning of the coming of a new thing among people. This is a revolutionary political mandate, for instance when a person decided to populate a nation or a community with people that are seen and considered fugitive to others to be tolerated among others. This is considered as a permissive mandate. Political mandate is either for a preventive or for a permissive motive or the combination.

Every political mandate has two important effects.

(i)   It has a source (ii). It has effect on the host community or nation.

Political mandate is an assignment divinely attached to a life for a motive, for instance, as in the case of Moses, and David in the scriptures. There are so many present and previous matters on which God is seeking for men and women to release them to. Without a life of purpose you are only breathing and not functioning. You are created to impact not just living.

Being given a political mandate is being given a role to play. A person is rated according to the role he or she plays; none is rated higher than the role he plays. You are a big role playing member of the society by virtue of your mandate.

Your political mandate brings you honor where your words become binding on those to whom you are set to deliver or save.

CHAPTER THREE

FUNDAMENTALS OF WINING IN POLITICS PART ONE:

1. **Divine direction: This means understanding what the will of God for you is.** Understand the spiritual truth about your politics ambition by your eyes being enlightened to be able to know your calling or mandate. Know whether you are divinely called into politics .It is not every candidate that is interested in politics has a political

mandate. Seek for divine direction by making inquiry from God's in prayers. Every person is attached a purpose. let me tell you here that it is of this purpose I am born. Seek for a direction. Divine direction is to be possessed by God and to hear from him. It means to let to take owner of your life driver's seat and emotion, and hearing him when he tells you 'go ,you go, and when he tells you do not go to the right or to the left you heard and obey, meaning God taken the lead and possession of your life. Then he tells you go to the right, to the left and you go. Seek divine direction. You can only hear from God when you are in good relationship with him. Do not distance yourself from God. Do not go away from God. It is only God that can open a door no one can shut up.

2. **Have a Source:** Everything has a source. The source of what you have is more important than that thing itself. Join forces together. The father, the son and the Holy Spirit is my source so who your source is very important. Your source has everything it takes to

bring your mandate to a reality. When you consult your source, He sends enough assistance to back you up. God always bring to us those He has by himself chosen or foreknow to help us. This divine help is a seal of his love for those that trust in him E. g,

- Daniel Source was God

- David Source was God, Moses source was God and it was God that led Jacob alone. Your source makes the difference in the result between you and your parallel competitors

Let us also see this backing in the instance of Saul and David or very shortly, in the ways of Jacob and Esau. God says Jacob have I loved (Romans 9:13) this was not with empty voice but in action God proved this love by helping him in all his challenges. God help marked the difference in the result between the two brothers and its terminate every unnecessary struggle. Constant consultation from your source delivers you from fowlers, shame and defeat. You consult your source by faiths, by committing Him to his word.

You don't break down when your source is strong. You do not suffer harassment when your source cannot be harassed. You cannot be intimidated when your spiritual back up is strong and heavy. When your source is not too heavy to carry, you will be too light to be carried

3. **Have A Company of Right People:** Those you have around you matters. This should be a company of right people. Your relationship should carefully be considered and be under a good watch. The relationship you keep

can pose a threat to the fulfillment of your mandate or destiny. Do not be careless about the kind of people you bring to your life, table of discussion and in decision taken. Every person is permitted to be in your group but not every decision. Involve a company of right people. Your right company ensures there is a sense of availability for programs and also pray time to time to see that you stand and succeed. Oneness has to be evident. Where there is oneness everybody sees it.

4. **Pay The Necessary Huge Sacrifice:**
You have a very huge scarifies to be made. Discipline is this huge sacrifice. It is either you do this sacrifice or you leave it. the areas you need sacrifices are:

    a. Discipline: Discipline is putting your tongue, your stomach, your body and feet under careful watch and control. Have no go areas. Being discipline makes destiny great

    b. In giving: Be liberal and cheerful

c. Integrity: with little or no integrity you go nowhere in life.

d. Shift from being manly to godliness and shift from playing to praying.

e. **Stop telling lies but the truth:** Never promised people what you know you cannot do. Your political mandate is either preventive or permissive. It is a calling for a special assignment. Little lies can easy destroyed a very promising career or future

5. **Give yourself a name:** A good name is better than big money. Give yourself a good name. Know who you are. If you know people and you do not know yourself you go nowhere. Whom you know do not matters as you. It is who you are that brings you what you need. "Give yourself a name" the name you give yourself terminates mockery.

6. **Built up your confidence:** Be confident. Confidence let you make sound. Return peace for peace and you return threat to a threat. Make sounds. The enemies will always behave according to the

sounds you make. Your sound determines your enemies' strength and behavior. Be bold enough to cut the camel's head through the power of your word. In the light of the above, your political mandate will be handed over to you to exercise authority and effect positively in your state, country and in the world at large.

7. **Be Focus:** Your total attention or commitment is needful. Focus is a daily commitment to running the mandatory race. Focus Polish and smoothing our course. Focus teaches and encourages

having the knowledge of your mandate; study it, learn it, say it, live it, pursue it and share it.

Focus is a very important tool in pursuance of a given mandate. Your focus defines your commitment. People want to see how committed you are. People also assess how far you can go through your commitment. There is no responsible man on earth that is ready to be a company of the un-focused. Be focus and you will have company of right people.

8. **Chose a Platform** for the Execution of Your Political Mandate. Have a political platform

9. **Plan what to do:** Your political mandate may be threatened or stolen. You cannot be defeated when you are mandate but it can be stolen from you. This is the reason I have advised you severally in this book to also get prepared by creating allowances for every unseen future or risk that may arise. I know with the knowledge you have received in this book, nobody will defeat you by stolen your mandate.

God will direct you on what to do on every confrontation.

10.   **Build up yourself in faith:** Build up yourself in faith. Without faith we can do nothing. faith can lead you, and also sustain you. Mandate is planed, and executed through faith. Political mandate as to other kinds of mandate are executed by faith. Faith lets you keep focus and to always be in charge of affair. We come out boldly for the calling by faith. You follow people by faith, and people follow you by faith. You also wine by faith. No one has ever

won by using carnal weapons and sustain it. It is through faith. Be selective and careful in the kind of weapon you chose to deploy in your political mandate pursuit

11.   .

Know Your Right mandate/calling Platform: Every mandate has an area. Political mandate has an area approved for its manifestation. It is specific. If you are approved to be chairman know it. Do not go for governorship position when God has mandated you for presidency. You can be president or vice president when you are mandated. You do not have to be governor before you are a president. It may work for others and not you until you are mandated you cannot be un-defeated. Know your placement. Political mandate is not a guess and do work.

12. BEWARE, BUT BE CAREFUL FOR NOTHING:

When you know you are walking in the truth, be careful for nothing. But you should beware of the following:-

A. Do not give in to maltreatment and intimidation. Sometimes this may not come from far unfriendly friends and unbelievers. Man's enemies may rise from his home. Some of them may be doing things without sincerity to add sorrow and affliction to your pursuit. Don't allow any of those things to move you. It does not matter what people say or do to bring you down but be focus and face your daily task with full commitment

B. Do not give into names calling. Beware! Do not turn back and give up for those who will not give up for you. Build yourself on a solid foundation.

13.   Beware of your tongue:– Tongue triumphs. There is power in the tongue. Let your yes be yes to issues that deserves yes. Let your no be no to the un-needful. Say the needful and keep your lips away from the un-needful. Beware of your tongue. it can either destroy or save you.

14.   Timing: Timing here connotes knowing when it is appropriate to do something. A vision exposed before time or too late can be destroyed. With time an enviable task is performed. Timing is very important even when

God open heaven for someone on an area of assignment. Timing is to inquire or knowing when to go about it in order not to destroy what you would do in your life.

One of the reasons I wrote this book is to minimize the crazy way people goes about in politics, power, and killing one another. Killing in the name of politics is repugnant to natural justice and to the common law.

I do not want to be seeing and hearing this again living a lousy life because of politics.

Wait for your time. A political mandate works with time. As a matter of fact, you will begin to see that things are not working at pace of time. You will begin to see set back and your age mates or colleague in the same mandate or career with you flying higher, but know that they have waited for their time so you wait for your time also. Note that waiting/timing is to enable you to prepare and to do the needful before you come out to run the race.

Chose to come out and pursue when everybody is almost tired of your parallel competitors or oppositions and you will certainly win without stress. The period of waiting or timing is when to learn how and when to win.

Political mandate is cheap to obtain if you can pay the price of waiting.

Every mandate from God in one's life will first tarry, brings us down and shaking up first and begins to promote us. We must face and accept the waiting experience first. This waiting is a firsthand experience we must go through in every divine task whether political or non political, preventive or permissive.

Timing/Waiting makes your mandate subject to right security, scrutiny and leads you properly.

May God give you understanding. May your waiting not turn to permanent delay, sometimes a delay that causes discouragement.

We wait for our time for it is better to wait or to delay than to be fast and killed the vision prompt. This waiting is not a permanent waiting experience.

CHAPTER FOUR

WHAT TO DO WHEN YOUR MANDATE IS BEING CHALLENGED:

1. **Pray and watch:-** Do not close your eyes as you pray, prayers works and makes the difference

2. **Still stand and be focus:** Do not suddenly quit. Also keep your focus

3. **Go back to your source:** Your source has everything it takes to keep you on track and to bring your mandate back to you. His help is always needful. Constantly consult your Source. Your Source delivers you from avoidable

mistakes, shame and from defeat. God

is our Source.

CHAPTER FIVE:

The FUNDAMENTAL OF WINNING IN POLITICS PART TWO:

(1). **Right attitude** is the pathway to fortune and success in politics. It does not happen by chance or luck. It is by taking meaningful and constructive steps towards a convincing desired for an end.

Entreating wining and support is by showing kindness to people around you. What you do to people is a pointer to where you will place them in your heart in politics.

(2). BE GOAL ORIENTED:

Political success begins with having a goal that is defined in your agenda. That is the reason successful men in politics are referred to as goals setters. No one get a goal except he set one. When there is no agenda there is also no purpose. Political ambition without a goal suffers frustration and setback.

Have you ever seen a basket ball match without a basket goal net? Without, the match will only end in frustration. If you are into politics without agenda you are in to fail and also ready to be wasted because you are going to lose money, time, and energy and being frustrated. This is the reason a political candidate must plan well before he opt in. Your agenda makes people to follow or to repel you.

Be a great goal setter .There must be an end. Let people know fully to this end I am contesting and for this cause I am called to politics with which I bear witness and is the truth.

It is not enough to have a goal as it is more important to have accomplishable goal details and the process. Understanding of the detail of your goal will place you on high demand in your political career. Great accomplishment is in outstanding goal set and a task undertaking with a strong desire.

Wining in politics is great, a long process; not short but quick for the prepared mind. We grow this Process to maturity. Until you are matured enough in preparation you don't go far in politics.

Create opportunity for wining if you cannot find any opportunity. Political opportunity is created by creative thinking. You can win even when others are seeing no possibility of winning. Say to yourself, I can do something here and truly presses into it to get it done even the chances are not there.

Be self inviting and attractive that hundreds man and woman can hold on to your pajamas, saying, "we will follow you.

It is your responsibility to do a search and get the information on where the politics calling gift in you can produce good result for your expected result. Conduct a research about where you must win. It is not everywhere people are that count in wining in politics. Conduct a research on where you can win and deploys machineries to there for winning. Look for where and how you can take over densely populated areas.

There are wards or zones you need concentration most, and when other places fail to give you votes, you still win

(3).YOU NEED ENDURANCE:

The law of endurance is a law in order to succeed in politics. It is a price you pay to win. The precious do not comes out o pressure. How much heat you are willing to bear today determines the higher you go in polities.

Many people are not willing to endure the furnace of the pressures of wining in polities. Winning is not as quick as fast in other businesses. Endurance is a required quality for distinction in politics. With endurance you can make out the most of your political career and not lose out. It takes a great price to secure a great destiny. Pay the price of endurance. Okay?

(4) BE STRONG IN WISDOM AND MEEKY:

The strength being referred to here is the place of wisdom, not physical strength to twist others or opponent's hands. A sense of purpose is upon the wise. Be adequately enlightened on your vision and mission mostly when you are stepping into politics.

Wisdom makes you unbeatable, unstoppable and undefeatable in your political career.

How can you get this wisdom? Check everything that is said by God and know it with meekness. Most things I have and do are not a result of my intelligence or physical strength. It was a result of wisdom of God and meekness.

If you want to succeed in your political calling you require meekness to see your greatness.

(5) JOIN FORCES TOGETHER

Enter into a covenant with God, "tell God the reason you must win. Tell Him what you shall do for Him.

Make Him know that the heart of every leader is in His hands.

The secret things belong unto the LORD, but those things which are revealed belong unto us forever. Power/ Leadership belong to God. Leave that opposition that say, "Over my dead body, you will not be there". Except it is not the will of God. Nobody can truly be your political father except God.

You therefore need the spirit of revelation that delivers to you cheaply what you need according to God's will for you. A revelation comes to those that are close to God. The spirit of revelation reveals to you where to go, what to do, what to say, when and teaches you how to win. So, engage the search light ministry of the spirit of God. Join forces together by entering a covenant with God and you will achieve.

You may think it is a joke when I say, there are things freely given to them that are in covenant with God.

This covenant cheaply commands the miraculous for live. Note! The insight and hindsight you need to fly high do not come by mere hearing and through political god fathers. They come through revelation. Remember that God can not reveal something to somebody without a purpose. When you walk on the revelation knowledge of God you do exploit.

(6) CONQUER CONTROLLING POWER:

There is a Law of sin at work on the earth. Forces have been joined together in darkness and have been left loose from hell to hold man bounds in sin.

There are control forces in the air that control people, make them to do things they never intended or wish to do. These forces will welcome people and begin to remotely control them, subject and bring people into captivity. Many are crying and sharing secret tears because of their approach and methods in their quest for political power. Making them do things they never intended to do e.g.

joining a wrong group that sees opposition as a cow for politics sacrifice.

You must be strong enough to conquer those control powers in air. There are many things you never intended to do, but somehow along the line, some forces take advantage of your ignorance. Don't be a politics person under the siege of sin! It is a snare.

The mission of dead spirit is to make men walk in all manner of unseemliness. This is the reason you need to be aware of what you may likely face in and out, from different people when on a track to be in charge.

There is what is known as unclean spirit. Every man you see reacting against the word of God because of politics has this spirit. This spirit commands the activities of the lust of the flesh. It collect, monitors, supervises, control, Co-ordinates and manages ungodliness. The unclean spirit is the spirit of the flesh:

Death

Wideness

Bribery and corruption, Politics itself is not a dirty game. It is men.

(7) HAVE A VISION AND INTEGRITY:

Where vision is, accomplishment comes. Having a vision is a catalyst to success.

There is no rigor and fear in pursuing a vision you mean. Note! If you have a vision, people will know. No one is ready to follow a man without vision except another one without it.

It is only a fool that dispute the needs for a vision. A lack of vision can fade someone's promising career. Vision gives direction. It comes from God; but you secure it.

Vision is an individual affair; it is not a collective affair. A man who has a titanic vision separates himself from every distraction.

Integrity: It takes integrity to enjoy politics. You must also first be free from every form of financial corruption. Be disciplined.

Be upright and perfect and be one that fear God, and eschewed evil begotten

Wealth and riches

If integrity is not put into place in your life, don't expect a   lifting in your political calling.

It is either you have integrity or you don't have it. Integrity should be 100% sure. If you don't have integrity, you don't have integrity. It is either you have it or you don't have it. Simple!

Do not promise your people what you cannot do; there is no integrity in it. When you are not faithful in word, who will commits to your trust the economy of a nation. Incomplete integrity is as not having integrity .Half integrity is the same as not having integrity.

Service: Be service minded. Let everybody know that your intention is to serve your people and truly be a servant.

To be service conscious and mindful is another good quality people look to. Success answers to service. Even Satan knows that there is reward in serving peoples acceptably.

And you shall serve the lord your God and He shall bless they bread and thy water and he will take sickness away from you.

Serving people fine is an indemnity against failure. Give to the needy and to God and honor your parents as well. Provide for your house hold and people around you and pay your workers well. Those things are noted unknown to you.

(8). PREPARE YOURSELF:

Preparation brings desire result in politics. You must be reasonably prepared physically and emotionally. You need to prepare because the unprepared minds are taken unaware by the prepared.

Preparation enables you to successfully and contagiously guard yourself against the entanglement of the wicked forces of this world. No one considers the un- prepared mind. Every outstanding result is traceable to outstanding preparation.

THE AREAS YOU NEED PREPARATION TO ESCAPE SNARES:

1. Social life

2. Spirituality

3. Finances

4. Integrity

1. Social life includes speech, outlook, relationship framework, etc.

2. Spirituality. Join forces. Spirituality here recommends God for you. Be sincere in whom you serve. Whom you serves and worship determines how you serve people. Spirituality also entails:

1. Prayerfulness

2. Honesty

3. Reliability

4. Fasting

5. Purity

(9). SOUND FACTOR:

There are thing you must do if you must overcome whatever difficulty you may face or confronted with. One of such is your polish and authenticated tongue.

The Sound factor is to be original in your quest for pulling crowd. Without attractive sound you are, but a wind.

The words you speak or produce also determines your waves and it is among your destiny building pillars. You can give color and meaning to your career or life by the sound you produce. Speak well, decently and say what you wish to say with conviction. The terrors in your front can be forcefully be subdued by your sound. Your sound is your instrument of command and the attention you receive from men.

Your word is great; make it strong and acceptable and forceful with its power.

1. You are your word

2. God confirms your word

3. Your words put other to work

4. Every of your word is a seed, & it will grow.

5. Your word can compel people to follow you or disperse them.

6. Think about your word for a moment. Stop if it is not needful and only say it when needful.

7. Your word should be so strong and compelling .Anything you desire is stir up by your word. Your word speaks about you. Speak **boldly** and rule your word. Speaking boldly gives authority to your speech.

Boldness is a proof of your confidence and the confidence people will have when representing them. Your confidence authenticates your speech.

Do not just speak boldly; but with trust and confidence that you will do what you promised to do.

Note! The more you know, the more you increase in strength .Nothing enhances confidence as knowledge (the power of your brain).

Boldness connotes depth of knowledge. Your word is the worker of the miracle you need.

Train up yourself: You should exercise yourself, that is, train yourself. Training is a must and also exerts effort to maintain a conscience void of shackles/ errors.

Having a good outlook and output and good conscience humor is not a thing that just happens one day you get trained to obtain it. We will easily succeed in an area you are trained.

(10) HONESTY:

To have good and pure disposition and conscience in a correct environment seem impossible and look like big impossibility. Honesty is an area to also be well trained .Honesty is a proof of a good conscience in politics and in other mandates.

With a good conscience you will not need any supervision to do what is good and right. Your conscience personifies and gives you dignity.

Good training helps to package you. It checks you when nobody is ready to check make you. From the time of cave to date I discovered that greatness in polities is rooted in possessing a good conscience else it becomes threaten and miserable.

Embrace honesty. Don't have anything to do with corruption. The wicked shall not go unpunished. Judgment hand will one day hang on the neck of evil doers (corrupt ones)

Expose evil doers. Expose them and make them known, then you free your conscience.

The world is waiting for you Sir: Build yourself to be envied, to be person of attraction, a person of honor, and by this you will storm the world. Build yourself as a person of depth knowledge, as a revolutionary army, and with this, you will take the world by storm and you do not need someone to announce you. My prayer for you is that the world should hear you solving problems.

The reason you come out is for God to support you and to give you the power to lead his people in your World. On their support you are to give them a purpose and fulfilment. Teach them how to do exploits and make them a generation of good people by your works or hand written.

The effectiveness of any person or a politician is determined by the quality of his or her training. So we have to train up in the power and secrets to political success for a meaningful development.

(11) BE WATCHFUL AND TIMING:

Have watchful moments. In polities, there are sometimes you watch. Just be watching when you do not suppose to talk mostly when it will hurt those that suppose to support you and bit your gong and drums for your announcement.

Watching conditions your foresight and insight to see and hear better. Watching sometimes helps us to receive signals i.e. sensitivity. Set yourself on a watch and you will see your opposition's plans and strategy will suddenly be revealed for your advancement.

Watching is sometimes helpful. You become alert to taking over. If you rush in..., you will rush out!

Be timing. Everything always has a time element in it. Correct timing is very important in everything. The race has an appointed time for its execution. We don't just begin to run a race because we see others running the same race. Know your appointed time because it gives safety, protection and straighten crook ways.

There is always a time for every political calling. When you come out at the time everybody has to do away with the opposition, then you will certainly win. Always know the appointed time and walk in with diligence. _In reality, no one wants to be an option, but in politics you come in when you are the only option. Seriously monitor this._

Timing is very important in any vision. If you come out at the wrong time and you miss it you will fall down flat.

In every vision, time comes when you will begin to know it is time to come in. Every vision is for an appointed time.

Everything has it time. Take off the plan from the board if it is not yet an appointed time.

(12) GETS USEFUL INFORMATION:

When you invest your time in getting relevant information that will help drive your vision, you will get result.

It is one thing to know where you are going and another to know how to get there, and it takes another effort to make use of what you get there.

If you lack information on how to get there, you will also lack information on what to do there and frustration comes in. Information whether spiritual, secular is the hubs of every outstanding accomplishment in politics. No matter your goal, information is a catalyst for its accomplishment.

(13).YOUR GROUP OR ASSOCIATES:

There are associations you keep to weigh yourself down and some will let you act speedily in your vision or calling

There are certain people you have to leave, separate from them so that you go far in your vision and experienced fulfillment in your pursuit.

Friendship is by choice. It is left for you to decide the kind of people you bring closer to yourself. Choose your associates that will assist you in fulfilling your vision, not those who are spiritual police men to detain you from your pursuit.

Any one that has negative influence on your life is an enemy. Let them go for you to take off.

A wise man said, you are the same person you were ten years ago except for two things: the people you walk with now and the books you read. You cannot be doing something the same way and expect different result. There are certain people you must let go for you to go forward.

(14) YOUR FOCUS-CONCENTRATION:

Another factor that will enhance your possibility of wining is your focus. Another word for focus is concentration.

Give your vision a full attention when you know that vision is a realty or real. Thank God for your hard work, strategic planning, consistency and so forth. But none of this is a substitute to a sound vision.

(15) TAME YOUR CONSCIENCE:

Every man has conscience. Conscience is the invisible you, you alone in thoughts and in actions. Your conscience is seen as the life-wire of every destiny, how is it is how you see yourself and your career destiny.

Your conscience is you, and only you can relate with it. Conscience is your inseparable companion. It mission is to check mate you, and polish your destiny according to the conscience you tamed.

As a matter of fact, the healthier is your conscience, the better you become in life.

There are various conscience:

(a) **Weak conscience or vulnerable conscience:** this is a conscience that is acceptable to anything bad or good. It does not have don't go area.

(b) **A defiled conscience:** this is purely a corrupt conscience. It tune into only corrupt things. It has taken corruption as a way of life.

(c) Dead conscience: this is a scared conscience. Those with this kind of conscience destinies are closed. Dead conscience precludes good works.

(d) **Evil conscience:** This kind of conscience is tune to only evil things and shut out all forms of kindness.

(f) Pure/good conscience: This is a living conscience also called active conscience. It confronts evil instead of bowing to evil.

Show me a man with good conscience, and I will show you a man with a great future and love. If you do not have a good conscience towards men, you wouldn't have for yourself.

It is all over to you. Your good conscience is your only way to where you are going. Train it up.

(16) HAVE FAITH:

Faith is a must in order to win. Any work or career is not your true career. It is uncommon to achieve and receive anything from people or God without faith.

The truth is that the greater your faith, the higher you go. The first thing to do before you step out is to build up your faith on that your pursuit. It is one thing to be bold, fervent and it is another to be faith filled as you pursue your vision. Faith gives you courage of continuity even when others see impossibility and entanglements.

Let your faith be in place before you start anything and let it be renewed. The level of your faith tank determines the level of response and result you get.

(17) HAVE THE LIGHT:

Light is your guarantee for dominion in the world of politics. Light never lose in any conflict with darkness. When you are overshadowed or overflowed with light, you will be in command.

You need light to dominate in this world. Light connotes knowledge, understanding and wisdom. Light gives you dominion in all sphere of life and makes you a master over your opponents and enemies that says, 'you wouldn't get it or there". How enlighten you are determines the degree you fly and command.

THE SOURCES OF YOUR LIGHT:

(a) Through Revelation by staying close to God by His word.

(b)Through Joyful heart: Be happy

(c) By the truth: Always embrace the truth.

(d) Quality information: Quality information is like quality food. Eat quality information.

(18). HAVE A PURPOSE:

Everything that God made was made for a purpose. What is your purpose in politics?

God has a purpose for making you a Politian. The purpose was because he wants you to be a leader, a representative for the purpose of saving, guarding and providing for your people.

Many people live and die without understanding the purpose of God for their lives .when the purpose of something is unknown, abuse is inevitable.

Many lose their election because they do not have a purpose and thought it was all about money; but God sent you into the world as a Politian for a purpose. Purpose is your place in your country, state, local government, your town or village, in your family under construction and developed to be free from poverty and for peace .Do not frustrate your purpose by yourself. You cannot be mandated and still be defeated. It is all about you. You are the only one who can frustrate your dream and your purpose on earth.

Nothing you cannot win or pass except when you refuse to learn how to pass or win. It is those that are ready to win or pass that win. This politics rosary will teach you how to win and it is only those that know how to pass or win that wins. No devil or evil force can frustrate your life except you agreed.

This Book (Politics Rosary – The Fundamentals of Wining in Politics) will teach you how to win in politics and sustains your power within your tenure)

(19) CREATE GOOD TRACK RECORDS

A steward is for his master, but in the case of leadership, the master becomes the steward. Always strive to be a good steward. An ambassador is a niche of his master or to whom he represents.

A leader is a special kind of person that leads while others follow. A leader supposes to be a light in the darkness by which others see. When the light is blinking, its followers get blind and when a leader is in darkness followers are in vast darkness and beeps.

A good leader cares for the well being of his people. This is the secret to making a working team call the followers to do their very best for heart blowing progress we desire. But today, some leaders and the followers make no difference. If a leader is bad, it is assume that his followers are rotten.

Leaders are our examples, and they should always lead by good examples.

A true person character is known when he takes a dominion or given an authority. This attitude is the desired character that every leader should sacrifice worldliness on attainment for his followers.

We all know of many leaders in the world that had enough money, they attained high financial success status without honor. We all know there may be prime leaders that are lonely. We all know people who had 100 convoy cars, but today they lack honor. They have lost out like mush-room overnight. Mush -Rooms grow quickly overnight and decays overnight.

Life is not about gathering money into one's pocket, grasping here and grasping there for ourselves and children and building fences. Life is not only about what we have, but it also about what we do to others (impacts).

Someone can educate the whole world without having a classroom (a fence) if his/her intention is to create impactful values and make a positive impact. Success is not about gathering wealth without an end. Success is helping others to be progressive and successful, loved, happy and peaceful.

Some past leaders did the wrong things. Their today dream is to correct the wrong they did but they cannot again because no one ever eats his cake and still have it. *One might have stolen the public funds because of love of it, but it is insecurity and poverty. I see this serious wickedness.*

Remember! When someone is the only one that is rich among the poor thousands, no matter his generosity he may still be at danger so make others rich to be free from poverty and insecurity.

Now, I want you to free your mind. You might say this author addressing the Societal Problem (the evil call corruption) don't respect. We *are the subject matter in this book.* The change we want begins with us.

Regardless of whether we are rich or poor, smart or not smart, Ibo or Hausa, Yoruba or Niger Delta or Ibo, Fulani or Hausa , negroes or Hebrews and Arabs by nation, the one common denomination will all have is the same identity of being visitors in this world. No one claim monopoly of the earth. We want the World to be great and be peaceful.

The problem we have today is much worse than it has been because of the inept attitude and corrupt practice of leaders and followers.

I keep asking:

Which tower will you build to the sky? Which estates, private jets, or whatsoever name is it called that has never been heard? Remember that we are going back to the soil with nothing because we came here with nothing.

We need good leaders.Not necessary saints from birth but also those that have run around and finally learned a good lesson. A leader is a role model that guide and lead others to progress.

Let us try to start thinking as nations, as individual than to slowly sink into an ocean. Let us not succumb to <u>big group-think</u> approach, which is just a bad way of sinking our nations into the deep ocean.

What Africa needs are good leaders. What Nigeria need is leaders and followers with a dream. What is our dream!

Our dream for now is to be free from corruption. If Nigeria will be free from poverty, it must first free from corruption, and then the world will rise.

The reason the world has not risen and settled is because Africa has refused to rise.Africa is the center of the whole world.

CHAPTER Six:

HOW TO GET FAMOUS/ POPULAR INTO POLITICAL OFFICES:

1. **Fear of God:** Fear the Lord your God and it shall be well with you. It was God alone that led Joseph to the second command rank in Egypt. In the absence of God, we can do nothing. With God, all things are possible (Ecclesiastics.12: 12). With the fear of God, we get all things we might ask Him for. In the absence of men; remember that there is nothing too hard for God. It was God alone that also led Jacob in the desert. Fear God in your office.

2. **Address Public Issues:** A wise man said, with that, I walked on stage to introduce my friend to thousands of families and students. Look for a person to take you to the stage of students, families, with the opportunity to address national issue politely without mincing words in what you believe you can do and have good result with accuracy.

3. **Learning: B**e an apprentice to a renowned and sincere person with your political interest. Look for supportive people who will push you to success? That is an opportunity for you.

4. **Have good negotiations skill and be patient:** Politica negotiation is not short and quick as in commercial negotiation. Have good negotiation skills with the patient to wait.

5. **Have a battle Field:** Every dream has its battle field. Fight your fight at the right battlefield for victory. Every victory is a plus for another victory that is yet to come. There is no dream too big to achieve. Have a battle field for your dream. That is it.

6. **Be personal:** Don't only depends on group thinking. Group thinking is good because it

sometimes pulls a crowd to you, but it should not always be something you do.

Break up the herd before you become incapable of seeing, hearing and thinking proper. Do it yourself. People who are capable of thinking for themselves will rarely be part of any herd or group thinking on a very sensitive decision.

Serious people stand alone on certain issues and win in argument; when they know they are right. This builds confidence on those that follows you. Only you should break camel's head.

7. **The Media:** The mass media is a powerful tool for good and for bad, so the bottom line is: you have to learn to think for yourself properly to forge ahead before the media think for you.

The media is very fast and universal. They float you or decide to sink you. Befriend them and be very careful with the Medias. Is it okay?

Make sure all social media channels are engagement friendly. This include your website, face book, twitter, go goo, and glass door channels. Don't promise what you are not sure you can do, and don't say what you are not sure.

8. **Have fans.** Fans are decorators and whirlwind that blows dust up and down for you. They go before you to clear radicals and thorns out of your roads for you to go ahead.

9. **Be Knowledge Based:** Have knowledge and truth based polity, with this you remain strong and unopposed. Nothing overshadows light (knowledge).

10. **Pray and Watch:** In all things put God first. Always pray & watch (don't close your

eyes when you pray. How do you see?), think and act appropriately. There is absolutely nothing God cannot do. With the above tips, you can become an elected leader and sustains it.

11. **Have clear goals, objective and commitment:** There must be an emotional commitment between the leader and followers which the followers engaged a leader for the country.

Followers need to hear why they should want to elect and work with you, why you are the best candidate for them, how they will feel when they elected you and work with you.

A country is only actively in support and ready to work with a person that excites and interests them.

Engagement in government service demands open communication of facts, clear goals and well understood objectives. Don't have the mistake of promising a person or groups what you are not sure you can do.

A leader must understand what the citizens think by using tools which include social media and online forums, encouraging open discussion and debate and giving people a voice. This is what great nations and personalities do.

(12).

HAVE A CLEAR PREVENTIVE MANDATE COURSE: E.G. CORRUPTION FIGHTING

As a Jew and a Bible person, I see corruption fighting as a Holy War. For it is written: *You will not let your Holy One see corruption/evil (Psalm 16: 10)*

Corruption is the saying and the doing of a wrong thing for personal benefit. What is not right is wrong and no wrong can make right.

Corruption is in every evil thought, word, and action that breeds evil result even when this evil motive is to get the right thing done. What is wrong cannot be right. Corruption is when someone is holding fast to what is wrong, and doing it for a selfish motive, e.g. bribery, looting, fake promise, aiding and abetting, lying pen, etc. To give a bribe is corruption and to receive it is another corruption. Any unrighteousness is corruption/evil.

Corruption is an unclean spirit, a force of ungodliness with the power and authority to fight godliness and inculcates all kinds of indiscipline, weakness and again using them to do more harm and damage with pleasure.

Corrupt person is someone that is saturated with every kind of unrighteousness, grasping and covetous greed, and is full of insolence, arrogance, an inventor of new forms of evil, disobedient, undutiful, and merciless.

It is not that such a person is not fully aware of the right thing and of God's righteous decree that those who do such things deserve to die. They do not only do them themselves but encourage, approve, and applaud others who practice them. This is a great evil on the land every leader and follower ought to resist and run away from.

KINDS OF CORRUPTION:

(A). *financial corruption:* This involves looting and stealing of money- directly or indirectly.

(B). *Corruption in words-* This is when a person is corrupt in words (Corruption of the word).Fake political promises is an instance of this kind of corruption. People with *good intentions make* promises, but *it takes those with integrity and the fear of God* to make them a reality and keep them. Don't promised people what you are not sure you can do. This is corruption.

(C). *Aiding and Abetting corruption is corruption.* Stop hiding evil. How can your worker be stealing without you knowing? Why are you a supervisor or a leader? We don't aid and abet corruption.

CORRUPTION OF THE WORD

Some people are not only corrupt in the way they go about finances but also in the word (corruption of the word).

Is it not because their heart and words are corrupt that they twist the law, policy, codes of conducts and given it a different meaning to suite their unhealthy desire? This stirs arguments, jealousy, and slander and brings division.

When a sincere person comes in to make things right, he will be called different names. To the spoiler, that kind of good behavior is a mere godliness and devil interface, and he is seen as a person who wants to be rich/wealthy and the spoiler's prayer point turns to evil prayer, wishing the person untimely death. Those kinds of people have an unhealthy desire to quibble over truth and cause troubles. Their minds are corrupt, and their words are rotten.

To them doing good work are offenses because it may stop their corruption, unethical behavior and their unprofessional way of doing things.

The Bible tells us to keep the mouth free from perversity and to keep corrupt talk far from the lips (Proverbs. 4.24). Do not be deceived evil communications corrupt good manners (1 Corinthians 15.33). This is corruption in the word.

Psalm 14:1 says, the *fool has said in his mind, there is no God. They are corrupt and commit evil deeds; not one of them practices what is good. Woe to those who call evil good and good evil, who put darkness for light and light for darkness, who put bitter for sweet and sweet for bitter! (Isaiah.5: 20).*

The original meaning of many words, policies, and constitutions are twisted to suite selfish interest. This is another form of corruption.

For instance, where is the proper federation of Nigeria as obtained in the 1960 and 1963 constitution? The constitution says Nigeria should be run along Federal lines to be able to curb impurities and to experience real peace. This has being twisted.

Is it not because the heart is corrupt that they twist meanings? Discrimination, tribalism, and racism do not come naturally; it is taught, planted and watered. This is a corruption of the word.

Religions heads and government leaders should desist from changing meanings. Leaders should stop telling lies, and promising us fake promises; this is another corruption (a corruption of word).

C. *Aiding/abetting corruption:*

Aiding and abetting of corruption is another corruption- This is when a leader or a follower is not supervising or being supervised, then watching each other activity in pretense as a leader or a follower. This is indiscipline; when we are twisting translations and interpretations of the word, policy, constitution etc. It also includes when someone turns back and closes eyes on people who are stealing and on that which deserves investigation for onward actions.

OBSTRUCTIONS /BARRIERS TO FIGHTING CORRUPTION

(1).The fighter must be healthy, knowledgeable, bold and financially balanced/ rich. If the fighter does not have money to fight, corrupt people may find victory.

(2). It is a long time fight and investment. The impact is not quick and seen in a short time; as a result, people do not cherish it.

(3). impatient: Many are not patient about fighting corruption; to them, it is a further waste of time, resources and energy.

(4). It is capital intensive since it requires restructuring and also blocking people who are corrupt into public offices entrance.

(5). It can lead to further corruption and violence if not jointly supported and handled carefully.

(6).A Perceived scam and dishonesty on the side of a leader by his/ her followers will aggravate further corruption practice that cannot be control.

CAUSES OF CORRUPTION:

- Indiscipline, Lack of integrity and principal values

- Lack of good leadership by good examples.

- Poor control and supervision of deligated duties and responsibilities

- Lack of vision, and high expectations due to over fake promises

- Lack of effective policies and regulations.

- A corrupt word corrupts people. Note! Faith comes by hearing. What is heard from the lips can build or destroyed

- Poverty

- Big gap between the poor and the rich, and sumptuous living...etc

DESIGN HOW TO FIGHT CORRUPTION AS A LEADER

- By teaching and preaching against it with good action example.

- Be a person of integrity and discipline. You can only do little things with some integrity and some discipline, but with complete discipline, you can do all things. Integrity is 100%; 95.99% integrity is no integrity.

- Start the change from yourself. The change we want must begins with us.

- Make every of your action plan a purpose driving one, and transparent

- Make clear your economic policies and let every body know your drives/intentions. You can write it in white and share it. This makes your vision clearer to those who read it.

- Be a true democrat so that you can carry oppositions along; but also learn how to stand alone on certain issues.

- Seek for supporters who are ready to drive with you the same purpose/ vision

- Listen to oppositions, their criticisms, and suggestions then take them to the screen and filter them because in every gossip there is something good to learn there from. It is not every word of an opposition that is meant to hurt. Stop pursuing oppositions any how.

- The essence of opposition is to validate our actions/lapses for our improvement. They contribute to our rising. Note, as they keep saying negative things about us, people step forward to see what we are doing.

- Appoint your oppositions and fix them in the areas they are complaining about to work with you. They Will not accept the work if they have evil intentions meaning that they are corrupt. Let them go so that you will not lose your F-O-

C-U-S. Always stand to what you believe. This is your confidence.

- Let their criticism and your action plan be your mirror to be able to measure your performance.

- Redeem your time (See: Jeremiah 8:8, Deuteronomy 31:25-29, 2 Peter 2: 15). There is no time at all to waste because people would like to see result per quarters.

- Test every thing and hold fast to what is good (1 Thessalonians 5: 21)

- Deliberate Repentance- repentance is not an option. It becomes a must for a leader to be able to rule with the fear of God and fight corruption. No one can out run God no matter how knowledgeable he may be

- Very stringent economic policies and laws should be made open to people in an expressly written form to avoid ignorance and seek support.

We have created an environment that accommodates ill -gotten wealth. This must be stoped. With this, we are fighting corruption without actually fighting it. Corruption is fought successfully through collaboration. It should be every body's agenda. There must be a sense of togetherness.

- Corruption should be seen as an illegal business by our government and take procurement policies serious. We should stop celebrating the wrong people and close the avenues and channels for cantering away with our money. Those that hold public offices should not have foreign domiciliary accounts without justification.

HOW TO DETER OTHERS FROM FURTHER CORRUPTION:

All unrighteousness is a big wound to a nation. It can lead to separation/ division since it ends in endless suffering, difficulties, and violence. How do we respond to/address such deep and gaping situation? The answer is in humility expected of a man as expressly obtainable in the word of God. The pattern for this recovery must involve the spiritual dimensions of:

- **Confession**- every looter/ corrupt man have to acknowledge the unjust and hurtful actions toward other people and the nation

- **Repentance:** Accept that you were guilty after confession, and turn from unloving actions to loving actions.

- **Restitution:** Meaning to restore that which has been damaged, destroyed and seeking justice with the authorities.

- **Reconciliation:** this is to express forgiveness which the repented sinner in turn received and now pursue intimate fellowship with God and men.

This is how to heal the wound infections.

Do not just go with the money, consulting profiled lawyers and asking for forgiveness without restitution. Restitution brings true forgiveness and reconciliation.

CHAPTER SEVEN

THE INJUSTICE IN WORLD POLITICS; AFRICA

Intense skin deep excruciating sacrifices involve in politics by some ruling cabal is primal. This is a naive demonic and occult approach to politics.

Politics is not design by God to take human life/ sacrifice in quest for governance.

Politics means government, and political affairs and it is for the masses.

Then, why should something not personal and forever takes you intense skin deep sacrifices? Remember therefore where you are fallen and repent and do the first work, else God will enter into your house and remove your crown and catch nothing. The word of God says, he that overcomes and keeps my works to him will I give power over the nations (Revelation 2:26). Political power belongs to God.

Government is for the people, and for their development. We must not be foolish. Don't pay hard to forget excruciating price for ant political position. This is injustice we do to ourselves resulting to horrific political demeanor due to long run heart blowing pain.

Isaiah 54: 10 says, my kindness will never depart from you.

Even when you do not win, you will remain the son of the highest God.

CHAPTER EIGHT

WHEN YOU HAVE DONE ALL YOU HAD TO DO

When someone is cordially positioned in God's original plan for him or her, he sees his glory and wins without or less sweat, just as the nose gets the oxygen without sweat or struggle. When someone is in God's master plan / agenda for him, he's stripped no honor and dignity. Someone can only be stripped off honor and dignity when not at where God has planted him or her. When you miss God's plan for your life, when you are on a course outside God's plan for you, you see shame, but when you are operating within his plan region for you, you become living testimony to your world.

Knowledge is no guarantees, neither are skills a security, Human smartness is no guarantee for this race. The battle is not for the stronger, neither is the race to the swifter, nor is favor to a man of skill. Being intelligent or knowledgeable is no guarantee for arriving at a destination. Rather it takes us father away from it.

It is about God's will for you. *When you have done the needful without the mandate what is the next thing?* God loves you without condition. Man cannot receive something or anything on earth when it is not given to him from heaven. The world is control by God and His forces being empowered for that. So promotion and exaltation comes from nowhere except from God. He exalts one and he brings down another. He made poor and he make rich. He created the clay pot and he made iron pot. He created a man and he made a woman. He created light and he created darkness. All are for a purpose. A political mandate is an assignment, a table for a preventive and permissive purpose. It is an undertaken, a task given to man to function in world politics. This authority is not negotiable.

When you are mandated, you cannot be defeated. Many people are into the work that is not meant for them. If you are not called, you may do all the needful and still not succeed. Even when you failed thank God because he is the reason you are not a dead person. Do you known the number of times you have escape death unknown? A living dog is better than a dead lion. That you did not win does not necessary means you were too wick, bad and evil or people hate you. NO. It can be that you are not yet mandated or approved so you rest and keep trying or you find where you belong to.

Most of my teachings on success generally, talk about what people should do to succeed.

However, many have done all the prescribed things. Many are doing what I taught, yet there is no positive change or a lifting in what they do.

Why is this so? The answer is observed; Promotion and divine lifting major on what people should do to succeed. I discovered that success is not so much a function of how much we do, how hardworking is someone, but a function of what God says of someone – destiny.

God is the judge; he putted down one, and He settled up another (psalm 75: 7).

Many are along doing what they ought to do well to succeed. Many are excellent in their field of endeavor, and some got opportunity passes them by. And they might also not have the required characters that match the work yet they are prosperous. Note! Your ambition or interest is far below what God says you should do yet you complain, in this scenario, we pray and find out God's purpose for us.

THE BENEFITS OF WINNING:

- You become a living testimony

- You become a good living example for emulation

- You become a key holder,(leader).He that holds the key holds authority.

- You have the opportunity to serve your people better.

- Your salaries will be enough to meet your needs and canter for your dependants.

- You become a world figure and being honored.

- Then you have all it takes to serve God better.

- You will feel fulfilled because you had the chance to champion a cause either permissive or preventive cause.

OTHER BOOKS WRITTEN BY THE AUTHOR:

- The Bowl of Treasures" (*An insight to light)*

- The Wonders of Grace

- Titanic Ideas (Think outside the Job & Your Employer's Box)

- Fame to Fulfilment (The Secrets to Achieving Fulfilment)

- Addressing the Societal Problem, "Corruption" & Creating Values in

www.ingramcontent.com/pod-product-compliance
Lightning Source LLC
Chambersburg PA
CBHW020238290526
45784CB00003B/1030